Think Like Jesus

What a great devotional resource from Dave Willis! I love the way each day's reading is encouraging, enlightening and challenging. Your life won't be the same after going through *Think Like Jesus*!

JIMMY EVANS
Founder and President of XO Marriage ✦ Apostolic Elder of Trinity Fellowship Church

---

I wholeheartedly recommend any book by Dave Willis. He's a friend, mentor, and a refreshing guide whose life joyfully spills out the wisdom found in the book of Proverbs. Want to live a life that honors God? It starts here. This devotional is thought-provoking and has helped me to experience the Scriptures in a new, fresh way. Make sure you grab a copy for a friend too!

RASHAWN COPELAND
Founder of I'm So Blessed Daily
Author of *Start Where You Are*

Dave Willis has written a truly wonderful devotional. This book will not only teach you the timeless wisdom of Scripture but will also reveal to you God's tender love and care for you!

ZACH MALDONADO
Bestselling Author of *Perfect and Forgiven* and *The Cross Worked*
Speaker and Pastor at Church Without Religion

We read this devotional together as a way to strengthen our faith and strengthen our marriage at the same time. The end result was life-changing. It has sparked many meaningful conversations which have greatly enriched our relationship and it also made us fall in love with the Bible again.

GARY AND SUSAN YOUTSEY
Married 37 years

Think Like Jesus from Dave Willis incorporates Biblical wisdom with practical application based on the life of Jesus. His wisdom and insight stems from many years of studying Scripture, both as a young person and an adult, and I believe it would be applicable for those in varying stages of life. With many years of wisdom, study, and ministry focused on marriage, he also gives practical ways to include your spouse in studying the Bible together.

PASTOR MARK DRISCOLL
Founding Senior Pastor, The Trinity Church

THINK
LIKE
JESUS

THINK LIKE JESUS

Timeless Wisdom from Proverbs

DAVE WILLIS

Think Like Jesus: Timeless Wisdom from Proverbs
Copyright © 2020 XO Publishing.

This book, or parts thereof, may not be reproduced in any form or by any means without written permission from the publisher, except brief passages for purposes of reviews. For information, address XO Marriage™.

P.O. Box 59888 Dallas, Texas 75229
1-800-380-6330
or visit our website at xomarriage.com

XO Publishing

All Scripture quotations are paraphrased by the author.

All rights reserved. No portion of this publication may be reproduced, stored in a retrieval system, or transmitted in any form by any means—electronic, mechanical, photocopying, recording, or any other—without prior permission from the publisher.

ISBN: 978-1-950113-52-1 (Paperback)
ISBN: 978-1-950113-55-2 (eBook)

Cover image © Shutterstock.com
Book design by *the*BookDesigners

XO Publishing has no responsibility for the persistence or accuracy or URLs for external or third-party Internet websites referred to in this publication and does not guarantee that any content on such websites is, or will remain, accurate or appropriate.

Printed in the United States of America

Dedication

This book is dedicated to my wonderful sons: Cooper, Connor, Chandler, and Chatham. Your Mom and I love you very much and we are honored to be your parents. As you grow, we pray you always follow Jesus and walk in the path of wisdom.

The Lord has wonderful plans for you.

"My sons, do not forget this teaching and keep these commands in your heart. They will add many years of peace and prosperity to your lives. Always pursue love and faithfulness. Keep them in your heart and you will earn favor and a good name in the sight of God and people."

PROVERBS 3:1-4

Contents

Introduction 1
DAY 1   Wisdom vs. Foolishness 5
DAY 2   God's Will for Your Life 9
DAY 3   Keep Moving Forward 13
DAY 4   Keep Pursuing Your Spouse 17
DAY 5   Work Hard 21
DAY 6   What God Hates 25
DAY 7   Wisdom Leads to Joy 29
DAY 8   Pride and Humility 33
DAY 9   Always Be Generous 37
DAY 10   Choose Your Friends Carefully 41
DAY 11   The Power of Your Words 45
DAY 12   There's No Real Success Without God 49
DAY 13   Peace Is Better Than Wealth 53
DAY 14   Teach Your Children the Path of Wisdom 57
DAY 15   Your Temper Is a Tempter 61
DAY 16   Pay Attention to the Right Voices 65
DAY 17   Protect the Powerless 69
DAY 18   Financial Freedom 73
DAY 19   Develop Your Skills 77
DAY 20   Don't Overdo It 81
DAY 21   Honor Those Who Have Sacrificed for You 85
DAY 22   Always Tell the Truth 89
DAY 23   Criticism Won't Kill You 93
DAY 24   Be Sensitive to Those Who Are Hurting 97
DAY 25   Learn from Your Mistakes 101
DAY 26   Don't Pick Fights 105
DAY 27   Let Others Do Your Bragging for You 109
DAY 28   Confession Brings Healing 113
DAY 29   Think before You Speak 117
DAY 30   God Is Our Protector 121
DAY 31   A Wife of Noble Character 125

Next Steps 129
About the Author 130

Introduction

Wisdom is often the difference between a successful life and a life that never lives up to its full potential. It's the roadmap that can give you a strategic advantage in every one of life's decisions. It's a pathway that will lead you closer to God and to the abundant life He has in store for you. It's the protective force safeguarding a home from many of the world's attacks and temptations. It's the foundation of a multi-generational family legacy.

Some people have misunderstood wisdom to be a mystical force that can only be attained by a privileged few. The truth is that God has made His wisdom available to all who will seek it. You don't need an Ivy League education or a fancy family pedigree. You just need a heart open to receive His instruction. He doesn't want His timeless truths to be a mystery to any of us. He has spelled it out in His Word. The Bible illuminates the path toward Christ and all the blessings He has in store for us.

The Book of Proverbs is the Bible's most condensed collection of practical life tools. Every verse holds power to infuse your life with more wisdom. Since the reign of King Solomon, for the past 3,000 years, these words have guided people along the path of wisdom. Proverbs is a treasure trove of divine insights which can deeply enrich every aspect of your life, your faith, your finances, your relationships, and your future.

This book is entitled *Think Like Jesus* because these Proverbs would clearly have been a vital part of Jesus's upbringing as a first-century Jewish boy. You can see many allusions to Proverbs (as well as other Old Testament quotations) throughout His teachings in all four Gospels. Jesus's life, ministry, and teachings were deeply rooted in the timeless wisdom of the Old Testament scriptures. With each day's reading, I'll tie the lesson from Proverbs directly to one of Jesus's teachings. Understanding how the Old and New Testaments harmonize with each other will enrich your faith and your relationship with Christ.

As a teenager, I was challenged to read one chapter from Proverbs per day and complete the 31-chapter book each month. In the years since, Proverbs has become central to my daily Bible study. I've started my day by reading a chapter from Proverbs thousands of times over the past quarter-century, and this daily discipline has truly changed my life for the better. This devotional comes from those 25-plus years of studying the Proverbs. I hope these timeless truths from Scripture will impact your life the way they've impacted mine.

In the thirty-one daily devotions in this book, I encourage you to meditate on the daily Scripture, reflect on the thoughts I've included, and then take time to pray. If you are married, also take time to discuss the application points with your spouse. As you go through these devotions, ask yourself, "What should *I do* in my life as a response to this Scripture?" For those who are married, ask "What should *we do* as a couple in response to this Scripture?"

One more note: All the verses in this devotional aren't from a specific Bible translation. Instead, they are paraphrases written in my own words. Because Proverbs is a book of such simple, practical wisdom, it seemed appropriate to put it into common language. I hope doing so makes it easier for you to understand and apply this wisdom.

Meanwhile, I pray that this devotional brings you into a stronger relationship with your family and friends and a more intimate relationship with Jesus. I also pray that this devotional will foster an abiding love for God's Word, which will continue to shape your faith and your life after you've finished this devotional.

God has good things in store for you! Let's get started.

DAYS

DAY 1

Wisdom vs. Foolishness

> *"Obedience to God is the foundation of true wisdom,*
> *but foolish people hate God's timeless truths."*
> PROVERBS 1:7

One of the main themes in the Book of Proverbs is the difference between a wise person and a fool. It might sound harsh to call anyone a "fool," but the Bible doesn't mince words. God wants us to know we have a choice before us daily: A narrow road that follows God's timeless principles of wisdom or a broad road of destructive foolishness, filled with every counterfeit option the world can provide.

We all have the propensity to be a "fool" in one or more parts of our life. Foolishness and wisdom have nothing to do with educational level, social status, or age. Fools can be young or old, male or female, educated or uneducated, rich or poor. You can't tell a fool from the outward appearance, but a fool will always reveal his or her foolishness through words and actions.

A fool lives as though he answers to nobody. A wise person knows we always answer to God and to the human authorities God has placed in our lives.

A fool scoffs at discipline and treats all forms of discipline as a prison.

A wise person welcomes discipline and knows it brings greater freedom and influence.

A fool can't be taught anything because he thinks he's already smarter than everyone else. A wise person humbly knows there's always more to learn, and every person, every situation and even every mistake can be a good teacher.

As we journey through the timeless wisdom in the Book of Proverbs, commit to yourself and to God that you'll study with a humble and teachable spirit. A humble heart and a teachable attitude are hallmarks of wisdom. Foolishness is the lie that insists you already know everything.

Allow the Scriptures to bring you encouragement and conviction where you need it. God's Word has a way of building us up when we feel broken, while revealing blind spots before they create unnecessary brokenness in our lives.

The path to wisdom begins with obedience to God. Some Bible translations of Proverbs 1:7 use the phrase, *"The fear of the Lord is the beginning of wisdom."* This refers to a reverent sense of awe, respect, and submission to God's holiness, power, and perfection. While we should indeed have this kind of reverence for the Lord, we should also remember that we can also approach God as a friend because of what Jesus has done on our behalf. We can boldly approach His throne of grace knowing He loves us and cares about every detail of our lives.

Wisdom requires drawing near to God through a relationship with Jesus Christ. Foolishness thinks we can approach God on our own terms.

Wisdom reminds us we are forgiven because of what Jesus did for us. Foolishness believes we must earn forgiveness and spend our life keeping score.

What would it look like if your life was guided by God's wisdom? It would look incredible! A life led by wisdom is God's vision for your life. Don't settle for anything less.

Wisdom vs. Foolishness

Prayer for Today

Father, thank You showing us the path to wisdom. In a world full of foolishness, You've given us Your Word to guide us in all areas of life. Please forgive me for the places where I've been foolish instead of wise. Please reveal to me the places in my life where I may be living foolishly without even realizing it. I commit to pursuing You and pursuing wisdom with my whole heart. Help me realign my life with Your Word. Show me how I can grow closer to You and how to become the person You've created me to be. Each day, help me identify and choose the path of wisdom, then help me guide my family on this path as well.

In Jesus's name, amen.

A humble heart and a teachable attitude are hallmarks of wisdom.

DAY 2

God's Will for Your Life

"Trust God with all your heart. Trust Him more than you trust in yourself. If you'll seek His will in all you do, He will show you which paths to take."
PROVERBS 3:5-6

These two verses represent some of the most famous and most quoted sections of Scripture—and for good reason. In life, there seems to be so little certainty or clarity. We're faced with countless daily choices. Some are mundane. Some could be potentially life-changing. As followers of Christ, we should seek to honor the Lord in every choice, but often we just don't know which choices are right.

Seeking God's will for our lives is about so much more than trying to discern whether God wants us to choose "Option A" or "Option B." We must remember that His primary will for our lives is to develop our character to become more like Christ, as we live in a healthy relationship with Him and with people. When Jesus was asked which commandment was the most important, He essentially said, "Love God with all your heart and love people."

Some people spend their whole life trying to figure out God's will, but that's not the best approach. The Bible never once tells us to "figure it out." But over and over it tells us to "trust God."

God already has everything figured out.

God's will for your life is for you to love Him, love other people and to become more like Jesus every day. His will is for you to be committed to your spouse and love each other selflessly and unconditionally. If we'll make these things our mission, then we'll already be living in God's will. We don't approach God only when we come to a crossroads and aren't sure whether to turn right or left. Instead, we spend our days walking every step with Jesus. Then, when we *do* come to a crossroads, He gently guides us toward the right path.

Even when we miss a step, He works all things together for our good. If our heart's desire is to know Him and grow closer to Him, then He'll be working His will in us and through us in every season of life. Should we rebel and defiantly choose the wrong path, He'll be right there to help us start over once we turn back to Him. He meets us where we are and guides us toward where we're meant to be.

Yes, God still cares about the details of your life. You should still pray and ask Him things like: *Which job should I take? Which house should we buy? Where should we send our kids to school? Which church should we attend?*

Yes, God cares even more than you do about the decisions you make, but most of all He cares about *you*. He doesn't want you living with anxiety, agonizing over every decision as if you're one missed opportunity away from ruining His plans for you. Remember that His will for you is for you to know Him and love Him. That can happen from any house, any job, and any zip code.

Start right where you are. Commit your current situation to Him. Promise to prioritize your relationship with Him and keep learning from Him as you pray and read His word. Choose to be thankful for your current situation, knowing God is bringing good things out of it—even during hard times. If you'll do these things, you'll be standing right in the middle of God's presence and His will for your life. If He needs to move you somewhere, He will let you know when and where in His perfect timing.

Prayer for Today

Lord, help us put You first. I know that's Your will for my life. Help me trust You with every decision. Guide me where You wish, and if your current plan is for me to stay right where I am, help me choose contentment. Use me here. I know my life is never "on hold," even if it feels like I'm in a waiting season. You're always moving. You're always working things together for our good. Thank You for loving me. I commit to trusting You with every part of my life. I commit every decision into Your hands. I know You're in control and will guide me where I need to go.

In Jesus's name, amen.

The Bible never once tells us to "figure it out." But over and over it tells us to "trust God."

God already has everything figured out.

DAY 3

Keep Moving Forward

"Stay focused. Keep your eye on the prize. Keep moving forward. Make sure you keep heading in the right direction and don't get sidetracked by sin or distracted by frivolous detours."
PROVERBS 4:25-27

A Thoroughbred racehorse is one of the most powerful and magnificent creatures on earth, but it has a significant weak spot. With eyes on the sides of their heads, Thoroughbreds have an extraordinary field of peripheral vision. In itself, that seems like a good defense mechanism. But it also results in all kinds of distractions. It makes it nearly impossible for the horse to run in a straight line or to keep its eyes focused straight ahead.

For a horse to run in a race, it must be highly trained. Racehorses wear blinders, which drastically limits their field of vision, forcing their eyes to stay focused directly ahead on the path. With training and focus, a Thoroughbred wearing blinders is capable of becoming an elite racehorse.

Humans have similar distractions. We don't quite have the same field of vision, but we are definitely prone to let our eyes wander. We're predisposed to get sidetracked. Normally, we might justify these small detours by imagining they won't make a significant difference. But we forget that we each are on a long journey. If a ship gets just a few degrees off course, it won't make a huge difference over the course of an hour. But during a transatlantic crossing, changing course over a few degrees can result in a difference of hundreds if not thousands of miles. It can mean arriving in Cuba when you were aiming for Canada.

The Bible admonishes us to run the race set before us, keeping our eyes on Jesus, Who keeps us on course. If you're following Jesus, you're always headed in the right direction. If you've gotten out of step with Him, even the smallest detours can create significant problems over time.

In life, sin can be what sidetracks us—especially when we pursue toxic forces and give in to temptation. Becoming sidetracked can also occur through more innocent missteps, like slowly allowing a career to take us away from our family. It can happen when we stop prioritizing a daily quiet time with the Lord.

Life gives us countless opportunities to get sidetracked, but God is always there to guide us back home.

Thankfully, Jesus isn't a cruel navigator shouting at you every time you veer off course. He's our loving friend and Savior. He gently corrects us like a good shepherd, patiently returning a lost sheep back into the safety of His care. Sometimes a sheep doesn't even know it's lost. Sometimes a person doesn't realize he or she is heading the wrong direction. Sometimes a marriage gets off course without either spouse realizing it. That's why you must regularly assess the direction of your life.

Take inventory of your life frequently so you'll be aware of any potential blind spots that might be pulling you off course and taking your eyes off Jesus. Stay in constant communication with God. When you have been sidetracked by sin—or even by an innocent oversight—ask Jesus to guide you back to the right path. He always will.

Prayer for Today

Jesus, please help me stay in step with You. Help my family and loved ones stay on the right course. Help me to follow You instead of going my own way and then asking You to "bless" my efforts. I know You're the leader; not me. When we're following You, we're always headed in the right direction. Please reveal to me the places in my life which are currently out of sync with You. Give me the wisdom and humility to surrender these areas to You and be willing to do things Your way. I know Your plans for me are perfect. Help me keep my eyes focused on You and the path of faithfulness before me. Give me the strength to walk with You—one step at a time—trusting in your leading and in Your timing.

In Jesus's name, amen.

Take inventory of your life frequently so you'll be aware of any potential blind spots that might be pulling you off course and taking your eyes off Jesus.

DAY 4

Keep Pursuing Your Spouse

"Your wife is a lifelong blessing and a precious gift. Celebrate her from your youth through your old age. Let her heart, soul and body continuously captivate you. Pursue her with all your heart for all your life."
PROVERBS 5:18-19

While this passage is written directly to husbands, it certainly has application for both husbands and wives. Even if you're single, the Proverbs' scriptures about marriage are important for you to know. By understanding God's plan for marriage, you're preparing yourself for a possible future relationship. You're also equipping yourself to encourage the married people in your life. These proverbs give you a glimpse into the close relationship Christ desires to have with us since we, the Church, are called "His Bride."

Of course, married people should be giving extra attention to these passages. When God's Word is the guiding force in your marriage, you'll be able to weather all of life's storms together. Marriage only works when you don't take each other for granted. The moment you begin to treat each other like "old news," you're sabotaging the lifelong love story God wants to write through your lives. Count every day together a privilege. Treat your spouse as a "lifelong blessing and precious gift."

There's also a sensual and sexual message within this Proverb. The Bible doesn't hold back when it comes to talking about sex. Even in this passage, the original Hebrew language contains a somewhat graphic phrase. In modern English, it roughly translates as, *"may her breasts always seduce you."*

Does that surprise you? Some Christians have wrongly assumed that God is prudish and sex is a taboo topic. Nothing could be further from the truth! God created sex and He wants married couples to enjoy it often. Sex is a gift that binds a husband and wife together on an emotional, physical, and spiritual level. The entire book of Song of Solomon—located in the Bible just after Proverbs and Ecclesiastes—is an uninhibited celebration of sex between a husband and a wife. That's right: The Bible has an entire book dedicated exclusively to the celebration and enjoyment of sex within marriage.

Prioritizing your sex life is also important because it safeguards your marriage from outside sexual temptations. One of the consistent themes in Proverbs is to warn us against counterfeit forms of sexual pleasure, which include adultery and lusting over anyone other than your spouse. Our world is full of sexual brokenness and sexual temptation, so guard your eyes from anything or anyone that might lead you down an unfaithful path. Sexual sin will sabotage a marriage faster than nearly anything else. It can cause immeasurable harm. Another Proverb warns, *"The person who commits adultery is an utter fool, for he wrecks his own life"* (Proverbs 6:32).

In marriage, we must simultaneously pursue our spouse sexually while also growing in purity and restraint toward the world's temptations. To improve in these areas, start by taking an honest self-assessment of your sexual thought life. Might any part of it be working against growth in your marriage? Think of any thoughts that might be harming you or your relationship. Repent of anything you're doing that might keep you from giving your spouse your very best. Ask God to guide you and help you adopt new, healthy habits.

Then, share with your spouse what you're wanting to do differently. Lean on each other for accountability. Mutual accountability is an important aspect of intimacy. Keep pursuing growth in your marriage.

When you're continuously pursuing your spouse, your marriage will always be moving forward in a healthy way. But when you allow your

Keep Pursuing Your Spouse

marriage to drift and you begin to take your spouse for granted, you're opening yourself up to temptation. You're also denying your spouse the wholehearted adoration and attention he or she needs and deserves. You are the only legitimate source of sex and romance on the planet for your spouse. Don't deny them that pleasure.

Give each other your best—not your leftovers. Be each other's biggest encouragers instead of each other's biggest critics. Speak to each other with tenderness and not with coldness. Keep pursuing each other. Remain captivated by each other. Never outgrow your passion for each other.

When you make your marriage a priority, it will become sweeter with time.

Prayer for Today

Lord, in a world of so much sexual sin, please keep us protected from temptation. Help us remain focused on You and on each other. Let our marriage grow closer with time, as we continue to pursue each other wholeheartedly. Forgive me for the times I've given my spouse my leftovers instead of my best. Today, I recommit to You and to my spouse that my marriage will be a priority. Bless our sex life. Thank You for creating sex and making it a gift to be enjoyed in marriage. Let our bedroom be the safest and most enjoyable place on earth for my spouse and me. I want my spouse to feel completely safe, secure, adored, and captivated by my love. Thank You for setting the example, Lord, by making us feel safe, secure, adored, and captivated by Your love.
In Jesus's name, amen.

God created sex and He wants married couples to enjoy it often.

DAY 5

Work Hard

"If you're prone to laziness, you should learn a lesson from the ants. Their work ethic can teach you some wisdom! They don't have a boss or a ruler to force them to work, but they still work hard all summer long storing food for the winter. Some lazy people spend more time looking for naps than they spend looking for productive work. Dodging work and sleeping during work time is the foolish path to poverty. If you live a lazy life, scarcity will haunt you and it will be your own fault."

PROVERBS 6:6-11

There are billions of people living in poverty around the world and many, is not most of them, are incredibly hard-working people. Their poverty is not a sin. In fact, Jesus repeatedly calls us to show compassion to those who are poor. He also challenges us to learn from the poor, who often embody spiritual maturity by trusting God to be their provider. For them, praying for their "daily bread" is not a meaningless exercise, but a necessity.

This passage from Proverbs and others like it are not meant to demean or demoralize the poor. Rather, these strong words are meant to challenge us to avoid a sinful "poverty" of work ethic. God wants us to rest when it's time to rest, but He also commands us to work when it's time to work. So many of life's problems will be solved if we don't worship work *or* rest. We must keep both in their proper place.

Hard work is not a punishment. Working hard and using our God-given gifts to be industrious can be such a blessing. Our hard work can provide for our families. Our work can create resources which enable generosity and fund Kingdom-minded missions. Our hard work can even be an act of worship. We're told in the New Testament to work hard at everything as if every task we complete is for God Himself, and not for human bosses.

Hard work gives us the grit and resilience to succeed in life. Hard work also provides a safety net to remove unnecessary financial stress. When we're disciplined in our work and disciplined in our finances, we don't have to fear the uncertainties of the economy. Like wise little ants, we've worked hard to save for the lean seasons. As with everything God commands, maintaining a disciplined work ethic is for our own good. It gives us—and our families—freedom and security.

Prayer for Today

Father, thank You for being my provider. All I have, including my ability to work, is a gift from You. Help me use the strength and skills You've entrusted to me to the best of my abilities. Give me the discipline to see hard work as a privilege and not as a prison. Help me realize that my work, when done with excellence and integrity, is an act of worship to You. Help me honor You and provide for my family through my work. While I know work is a good thing, help me never find my identity in my job—or my lack of a job. I know my identity is in You alone and not in my title, career, or income. Guide my steps to all the work You've prepared for me to do and help me do it with joy.
   In Jesus's name, amen.

God wants us to rest when it's time to rest, but He also commands us to work when it's time to work.

DAY 6

What God Hates

> *"God hates six things and seven things he truly detests: eyes that look down on other people, a tongue that speaks lies, hands that shed innocent blood, a heart that harbors evil motives, feet that run into sin, a dishonest witness who brings false accusations, and a person who intentionally brings drama and division into a family."*
> PROVERBS 6:16-19

God is the embodiment of love, so some people are surprised to learn in Scripture that God is capable of "hate." They scratch their heads in confusion. How can an all-loving God hate anything? The Bible teaches us that it's precisely because God so fully loves His children that He's able to so fiercely hate those things which harm his children.

In this list from Proverbs chapter six, we see a list of some of the things God hates. This is a window into the mind and heart of our loving heavenly Father. Each listed item is an action which directly harms God's children and attempts to sabotage His blessings for them. Each item on this list hurts both the victims of the heinous actions and the perpetrators, who dehumanize themselves by devaluing God's laws and other people.

God hates eyes that look down on other people because He has created all people in His image with dignity and eternal significance.

God hates a tongue that speaks lies because it's the truth that sets us free.

God hates hands that shed innocent blood because He never wants His children to suffer needless harm.

He hates a heart that harbors evil motives because such a heart makes no room for Jesus, who is our only Savior and Lord.

He hates feet that run into sin because sin hurts everyone.

He hates a dishonest witness because false testimony perverts the path of justice.

He hates someone who stirs up drama and division in a family because God desires that His children live together in love and unity.

We are called to be people after God's own heart. This list of what God hates is more than just a warning of behaviors to avoid. While we should obviously avoid the hated attitudes and actions on this list, we're called to more than avoidance. This list helps us clarify God's plans and purposes in our own lives and in the world around us. If we'll continue walking with God and learning from Him, our hearts should be steered toward loving the things He loves and hating the things He hates.

As an example, this righteous anger within Jesus caused him to flip over the money-changer's tables in the temple and drive them out with whips. Jesus—the embodiment of love—was capable of this holy rage because He has the heart of God. His love for people caused Him to be enraged at behaviors that exploited people or erected barriers between people and God.

There are times when we should feel a righteous anger too. There are times when we should allow that anger to prompt us to act. When we see the vile exploitations of human trafficking, we should fight for the freedom of the enslaved. When we see lies perverting the course of justice, we should boldly declare the truth and be willing to fight to protect it. When we see injustices being celebrated, we should be compelled to sacrifice our own comforts to protect the justices of others.

An important caveat here is to remember that, while we should boldly stand on God's truth, we're not called or qualified to judge every aspect of the world around us. If we're not careful, we can fall into a legalistic pattern of judgment and completely miss the heart of Jesus in the process. This is what happened to the Pharisees of Jesus's day. They loved the rules more than they loved God. If a righteous anger stirs within you, let it be directed first at your own sin. Only then will you have the humble spirit necessary to remove the plank from your own eye before helping someone else take the speck of sawdust out of their eye.

> ## *Prayer for Today*
>
> Lord, help heal our broken world. We're overwhelmed by the injustices we see all around us, and we often feel powerless to bring positive change. Give us a courageous heart which loves people and hates injustice. Help me speak boldly when I need to and help me keep silent when I need to. Help me discern which situations require immediate actions and which ones require patience. Thank You, Lord, that one day You will set all things right and make all things new. Start by doing a work in me. Forgive me for the times I've done things You hate. Turn my heart completely toward You so I can be an instrument of your grace—bringing your kingdom, justice, and love to the broken world around me.
>
> In Jesus's name, amen.

The Bible teaches us that it's precisely because God so fully loves His children that He's able to so fiercely hate those things which harm his children.

DAY 7

Wisdom Leads to Joy

> *"Wise people are joyful people, so look for wisdom in all times and in all places. Everyone who finds wisdom finds life and receives blessings from the Lord."*
> PROVERBS 8:34-35

One of the greatest lies the world has ever believed is that the fun stops when you start to follow God with all your heart. This inaccurate stereotype of faithful Christians has been perpetuated by centuries of paintings and sculptures, all of which depict saints and Christian martyrs with solemn expressions and painful grimaces on their faces. This misconception of Christianity is dangerously inaccurate.

Certainly, the Christian life (and life in general) can be full of trials and pain. Jesus Himself even experienced great pains on earth, but He never lost His joy. As His followers, we shouldn't either. The Holy Spirit brings love, joy, peace, patience, kindness, goodness, faithfulness, gentleness, and self-control into the hearts and lives of all who follow Jesus. The Bible tells us the joy of the Lord is our strength. It's a strength that is greater than any negative circumstances this life can throw our way.

Wisdom and joy might seem like two separate roads on the Christian journey, but this Scripture reminds us that they are both parts of the same path. The path of wisdom leads to joy and the path of joy leads to wisdom. As we seek joy, we'll also find wisdom. As we seek wisdom, we'll also find joy.

King Solomon wrote most of the Proverbs. The Bible tells us he had more wisdom than anyone on earth, but that wasn't the case his whole life. The wisdom entrusted to Solomon came to him as a gift. The Bible tells the story of young Solomon preparing to inherit the throne left by his father, King David. God told Solomon he could ask for anything and it would be granted to him. Instead of riches or power, Solomon humbly asked for the wisdom necessary to be a good and faithful leader.

God was so pleased with Solomon's heart for wisdom that he made Solomon the wisest ruler of all time—and then also granted Solomon great wealth and power. Because Solomon valued wisdom first, God gave him everything else in addition to the wisdom. Solomon was joyful and wise, and both his joy and his wisdom were gifts from God.

Tragically, Solomon did not always use his wisdom to make wise decisions. He was still prone to selfishness and sin. There were times he disregarded the wisdom God had given him and made foolish decision instead. He sinned sexually. He sinned with pride and greed. He sinned by allowing his heart to be led away from God.

By ignoring his wisdom, Solomon invited chaos into his life. When he chose sin instead of wisdom, he sabotaged his joy. Solomon experienced a lot of unnecessary pain and caused a lot of unnecessary pain by straying from the path of wisdom. When we stray from wisdom, we invite the same kinds of pain into our own lives. Inevitably, in the process, we will also lose our joy.

Thankfully, God is a God of grace. Because of Jesus, all our pain is temporary, and all our joy will be eternal. Once we confess our sin and turn back to Him, He forgives us and sets us back on the path toward healing. The healing journey can still be painful as we deal with the natural consequences our sin may have caused. But even in this discomfort, God mercifully leads us and bears our burdens.

Keep pursuing wisdom and keep embracing the joy God wants all of His children to experience. If you've strayed from the path of wisdom, you don't have to stay on the road to misery. Choose today to recommit your life to God and His ways. Embrace the joy He wants you to experience.

It only takes one moment to fall into sin. Thankfully, it only takes one moment to repent and get back on the right road.

> ## Prayer for Today
>
> Father, thank You for the joy You give to Your children. Thank You that You offer mercy and grace when we stray from the path of wisdom. Please help me stay on the right path. Help me live a life of joy. I know in a world with so much brokenness and superficial happiness, true joy points people to You. Help me embody the kind of contagious joy that turns the skeptical hearts of those around me toward wanting a life-giving relationship with You. Thank You for the wisdom and joy You make available to all who will follow You.
>   In Jesus's name, amen.

*As we seek joy,
we'll also find wisdom.
As we seek wisdom,
we'll also find joy.*

DAY 8

Pride and Humility

> *"Pride and arrogance lead to destruction,*
> *but a humble heart invites wisdom."*
> PROVERBS 11:2

Pride is a very different thing than confidence. As Christians, we should be the most confident people on earth. We should be confident in our calling. We should be confident in God's promises. We should be confident that God will never leave us or forsake us. Since our confidence is rooted in God and not in ourselves, we can—and should—be confident and humble simultaneously.

A humble heart is the only kind of heart where Jesus can take up residence. He won't compete with our sinful pride.

Pride is the arrogant voice that chases away correction, reason, wisdom, and even chases away God Himself. Pride convinces us that we don't need to listen to others. Pride puffs us up with an identity built on superficial and temporary circumstances. Pride is the undoing of relationships and the ultimate wrecker of lives.

Pride will ruin your life and then, ironically, make you too proud to admit you've committed any failure at all. Though pride is the cause of so much destruction, it blinds its victims to the real cause of their own downfall. Pride provokes the downfall and then manipulates the prideful person to blame the destruction on other people or factors. Remember: *"Pride inevitably leads to your own downfall"* (Proverbs 16:18).

Don't be quick to chase accolades or seek the spotlight. Allow God to put you in those places of honor according to His timing. Otherwise, you'll end up there with the wrong motives. Your pride may sabotage any good you could have accomplished with your influence. Don't go through life strutting around trying to convince others of your importance. Your importance is rooted in God, and He uses people who limp more than people who strut.

When you let go of pride, your hands and heart will be open to experience the full life of wisdom God wants you to live. When you give up the need to build your own image, you can be formed more completely into the image of Christ. When you surrender your need for control, you are tapping into the power of God to control your circumstances for the better.

Don't ever mistake humility with weakness. Jesus was humble and yet He was all-powerful. Humility is not weakness; it's strength under control. Humility recognizes we have authority only because we're under authority. When we stay safely under God's authority in all parts of our lives, we can walk in confidence, knowing His all-powerful authority protects and guides all parts of our lives.

Also understand that humility doesn't mean beating yourself up or devaluing yourself. On the contrary, seeing yourself through God's eyes is actually the highest view of a human life. Pride isn't a sin because it causes you to think too big. It's actually a prison that tricks you into thinking far too small.

When you do fall because of pride, remember you don't have to be defined by that defeat. Have the humility to admit fault, seek forgiveness, learn from your mistake, and start walking in God's wisdom. Pride may be the enemy of wisdom, but humility is the fast-track to wisdom.

Prayer for Today

Father, please forgive me of my sinful pride. Help me walk in the humility of knowing that You're in control. Help me walk in confidence, recognizing that confidence is actually a gift from You, while pride is a sinful counterfeit for confidence. Please help my heart stay humble and teachable. Thank You for Your presence in my life, and for guiding me along the path of wisdom. Please keep me on that path, and don't let pride ever sabotage Your plans and purposes for me. Help me have a heart like Jesus.

In Jesus's name, amen.

A humble heart is the only kind of heart where Jesus can take up residence.

DAY 9

Always Be Generous

> *"Generosity leads to prosperity. Those who bless others will themselves be blessed."*
> PROVERBS 11:25

It seems counterintuitive, but in God's economy, giving is its own form of receiving. The backwards value systems of the world tell you to *get* all you can. God tells you to *give* all you can.

We might think that being generous will lead to destitution, but godly generosity is a pathway to prosperity. Though financial blessings can be part of it, this "prosperity" doesn't just refer to finances. God's prosperity includes a richness of joy and peace that could never be quantified in solely financial terms.

Jesus was the perfect model of God's generous heart. Jesus sacrificed His position of glory and comfort in heaven to enter our world of brokenness and pain. He sacrificed the wealth of heaven for a life of poverty. He sacrificed His time on earth to serve the needs of others, instead of claiming His right to be served. He gave His life on the cross to pay the price of sin—a price that was our debt and not His.

In living a supernaturally generous life, Jesus received much more than He lost. He gave His life, but He was resurrected to an eternal life. He suffered temporary pain, but it paved the way for us to experience eternal glory with Him. God has a way of taking our generous gifts offered in faith and multiplying them like seeds in a fertile field. In the harvest, these seeds yield 30, 60, or even 100 times what was originally given.

Generosity also invites joy into your life. Think about the most joyful people you know. Odds are, they're generous people.

Now, think about the more generous people you know. Odds are, they're also joyful. Joy and generosity are like two wings on the same bird. Once you choose one, you realize the other is attached and your life begins to soar.

The Bible often challenges us to take an inventory of our own lives and choices. I want to invite you to do that right now regarding generosity. Have you been faithful in your generosity? Have you trusted God with the tithe, which is the first ten percent of your income? Have you helped those in need? Are you experiencing the prosperity and joyfulness that are the fruits of a generous life?

If that mental inventory made you nod your head in agreement, then keep up the great work you're doing in the area of generosity! But if that list made you grimace in discomfort because it revealed some growth areas in your life, don't beat yourself up. Start right where you are and commit to live more generously. Ask God to guide your steps in this area. Study on your own to learn the financial principles outlined in the Bible.

It's foolish to say we trust Jesus with our hearts but are reluctant to trust Him with our money. Remember, it all belongs to Him. We are only temporary stewards of our money. That frees us up to give faithfully when prompted. When we honor God and serve others by giving of our time, talents and treasures, blessings always follow.

Prayer for Today

Jesus, thank You for giving everything for me. Help me live my life with the same generous Spirit You have. Lead me and guide me toward faithful stewardship of my time and my resources. Help me be a blessing to others. Let me never love money more than I love You or more than I love people. Help my priorities stay in line with Yours. Please help me experience the joy and freedom that generosity always makes possible. Thank You for Your goodness and grace.

In Jesus's name, amen.

Joy and generosity are like two wings on the same bird. Once you choose one, you realize the other is attached and your life begins to soar.

DAY 10

Choose Your Friends Carefully

> *"If you want to be wise, then spend time with wise people. If you want to get into trouble, then hang out with troublemakers."*
> **PROVERBS 13:20**

One of the greatest distinctions between a wise life and a foolish life appears in how we choose our friends. When we value personality over integrity, we're being foolish. When we keep chasing after selfish friends—trying somehow to win their praise and loyalty—then we're wasting our energy. The Proverbs teach us that a true friend will stick to us closer than a brother. This is the kind of friend we need to be and the caliber of friends we need to seek.

Jesus was a friend to all, but He was also very intentional about choosing His inner circle. We must show the same intentionality. After all, your life will start to look like the lives of your closest friends. If you are choosing to spend time in the company of wise friends and mentors, you'll find that their wisdom is contagious. If you are hanging out with people of questionable character, you'll find that their compromised values will start rubbing off on you.

Choosing our friends wisely is not an excuse to become elitist or act like we're better than anyone else. In fact, the right friends should help us to become more humble and willing to serve others from all walks of life.

We are fueled by healthy relationships. When we prioritize time alone with Jesus and time together with close friends who share our faith and values, we'll become the best versions of ourselves. *"Just like iron sharpens iron, true friends help sharpen each other"* (Proverbs 27:17).

Our friends have profound influence in our lives, especially during moments of vulnerability and at crossroads in decision-making. Surrounded by the wrong voices, you might be encouraged to pursue a divorce when God is calling you to fight to save the marriage. The wrong voices might enable unhealthy habits when a true friend will provide loving accountability. The wrong voices might cause you to compromise your character—in a misuse of peer pressure—while a wise friend will help you achieve even higher levels of character and integrity.

To attract wise friends, we must first commit to being a wise friend. Start where you are by living with integrity at work, at home, online, and in all parts of your life. Wise words and wise actions attract others who want to live with wisdom. But when you speak and act with selfishness, foolishness, and a disregard for God's Word, you'll draw peers who share those same mindsets. Be intentional.

Staying on the path of wisdom becomes much easier if you have the right friends sharing the journey with you.

Prayer for Today

Lord, thank You for being my truest friend. Thank You that You never leave me or forsake me, even when others have. Help me be a true friend to You and help me connect with others who will be true friends as well. Give me the wisdom to discern who should be part of my inner circle. Help me choose friends who will increase my wisdom instead of those who might sabotage my wisdom. Protect me from negative influences and help me never be a negative influence to others.

In Jesus's name, amen.

To attract wise friends, we must first commit to being a wise friend.

DAY 11

The Power of Your Words

"Kind words diffuse anger, but harsh words instigate fights."
PROVERBS 15:1

Life is full of tense moments. From our everyday relationships and interactions to global leaders and diplomats try to solve international problems, words make a big difference. The tone of your words will shape the tone of your life. Choose a positive tone.

In Jesus's famous Sermon on the Mount, He gives special praise to the "peacemakers." In every situation, you have the unique opportunity be either a peacemaker or an instigator. Let your default mode be one of peace.

Be slow to anger. Be slow to take offense. Choose to believe the best in people and their motives. Look for common ground wherever it may be found.

To find common ground and diffuse tense situations, your ears are as important as your mouth. The more you listen, the more credibility you'll have when you speak. Pride may tempt you to shout until your point is heard, but the humble path to wisdom gives you the discipline to lean in and listen. Seek to understand even more than you seek to be understood. Seek to win friends more than you seek to win arguments.

Especially within our most intimate relationships—like marriage, family, and very close friendships—we must guard our words carefully.

We can't treat strangers and work associates with kindness and courtesy only to come home and be cold and critical toward the people who matter most. Don't take your loved ones for granted. Your words will either be a force uniting your family together or a divisive wedge separating you from your loved ones.

The Bible tells us that the power of life and death is in the tongue. Our words have immense power to tear down or to build up. God created the entire universe using only the power of His words, and then He created us in His image—giving power to our words as well. Use this power for good and not for evil. Be a peacemaker.

While our default mode should always be one of peace, there will be moments in life when we must speak up and correct others (just like when Jesus rebuked the Pharisees). In these delicate moments, we must simultaneously be humble and bold. Boldness is rooted in a desire for the truth to be spoken, even when it requires courage to say it. Humility comes from a sincere desire for even our corrective words to ultimately build others up.

If we'll allow the Holy Spirit to fill our hearts and guide our steps, He will give us wisdom with our words in the moments when we might not know what to say. If you live surrendered to God, then He will empower you with the wisdom you need in every conversation. Wisdom is not the same as eloquence, so don't feel the need to make your words poetic. Simply speak the truth and do it with love, and you'll be on the right track.

Prayer for Today

Father, thank You for entrusting me with such power and influence with my words. Help me use my words to build up and not to tear down. Please forgive me for all the careless words I have spoken in my life. I know I've done damage both intentionally and unintentionally. Please help me avoid causing pain in the future and bring healing to the damage I've already caused. Give me courage when I need to speak with boldness. Give me humility when I deserve a rebuke. Help me listen and learn instead of simply spouting off my own opinions. Thank You for the love and patience You have for me. Help me show this same love and patience to others.

In Jesus's name, amen.

The tone of your words will shape the tone of your life.

DAY 12

There's No Real Success Without God

"People are always making their own plans, but the Lord is the one who gives the right answers. People think all their own ways are right, but the Lord is the only accurate judge of our hearts and motives. Commit all your plans and all your work to the Lord, and He will be the one who ensures your success."
PROVERBS 16:1-3

Sometimes, people proceed with their own plans without even pausing to consider whether or not God might be directing them. They move forward with cavalier confidence, praying only as an afterthought. That's when they ask God to bless what they've already decided to do.

We've all been guilty of these kinds of broken mindsets related to God's will. Some of our mistakes come from an innocent misconception about what God's plans are all about. The good news is that God's will for your life is not as complicated as you might imagine it. Ultimately, He wants you to love Him, love other people, and develop your character to reflect the heart of Jesus.

God cares about the details of your life even more than you do. He loves you even more than you love yourself. When you come to big decisions, He wants to guide you—but He also wants you to realize those bigger aspects of His will. If you'll make it your daily mission to grow in your love for God and people while staying rooted in Christ, then the

Lord will be able to direct you toward everything He has for you.

When you are walking with Jesus, you're always headed in the right direction. Even if you happen to take your eyes off Him and get sidetracked, God's grace is there to help you get back on the right path. Yes, you still need to make plans. You need to make wise decisions, but you should always remember that God is working in you, and He is the One who will bring success. *"The warhorse is prepared for the battle, but the Lord is the one who brings the victory"* (Proverbs 21:31).

Prepare to be reminded that His version of success might look different than your own. The "success" He has planned for your life is more about your character than any specific outcomes or goals you've set for yourself. Even a season of struggle and disappointment can produce great "victories" in God's eyes, if those struggles bring you closer to God and make your heart more like the heart of Jesus.

Remain diligent in your work and in your plans. Hard work and smart planning honor God and put wisdom into action. As you plan and work, just remember that, ultimately, God is in control. He is doing a work in us and through us that's bigger than anything we could ever plan or accomplish on our own.

Prayer for Today

Lord, thank You for caring about every detail of my life. Thank You for loving me so much. Please guide me in all life's decisions. Give me peace about which way I should go. Remind me that Your will for my life is primarily about my relationship with You. Help me put You first in everything and shape my heart to be like Yours. I commit all I am into Your hands. Take my dreams, my plans, my goals, and my very life as an offering to You. I know any success achieved apart from You isn't real success. I want Your will and not my own.

In Jesus's name, amen.

When you are walking with Jesus, you're always headed in the right direction.

DAY 13

Peace Is Better Than Wealth

> *"Eating leftovers in peace is far better than a houseful of feasting with conflict."*
> PROVERBS 17:1

When you imagine your dream home, what do you picture? For most of us, we're conditioned by TV shows and social media to dream of a home with opulent finishes, spacious yards and immaculate cleanliness. While those physical attributes of a house can bring certain comforts, the Bible calls us to a much richer vision of home-life. We're reminded that a shack filled with peace and love is infinitely better than a mansion filled with strife and drama.

We all have a responsibility to foster peace in our homes. For those of us who are married, we have an added responsibility of bringing peace to our marriage. The tone of a marriage will ultimately shape the tone of a home—and Proverbs has harsh words for any husband or wife who don't value peace. For instance, *"It's better to live alone in a dusty attic than to share a beautiful home with an unkind spouse"* (Proverbs 21:9).

While we all desire peace in our homes, peace can be an elusive quest if we don't go about it in the right way. We tend to think of peace as the absence of conflict. But Proverbs and the Old Testament scriptures use the much richer term *shalom* to describe peace. *Shalom* is much more than a lack of conflict. Instead of the absence of something, *shalom* is about the presence of something: God's authority in our lives.

We will experience God's peace when we make Him the authority over every part of our lives. His authority brings protection and wholeness. Without His authority, we exchange wholeness for the chaos that reigns whenever God's laws are not being followed.

Take an inventory of your life, home, and relationships. Identify the areas where chaos has a greater foothold than peace. Which places are more defined by brokenness than wholeness? Those are the very areas where you must declare God's authority, and invite Jesus, the Prince of Peace, to reign supreme. When Jesus guides your words, thoughts, actions, motives, and relationships, you will enjoy peace in your home.

Finally, it's important to recognize that the presence of peace isn't a guarantee against conflicts or even tragedies. We still live in a broken world and the storms of life will rage against us at times. If your home is firmly fastened to a foundation of faith in Christ, your home will endure life's storms. Even through tears and scars, God's peace can continue to reign supreme in your heart and your home.

Prayer for Today

Jesus, I invite You to reign as the Prince of Peace and the King of Kings in all parts of my home and my life. I know I can't truly experience real peace or sustained peace without Your presence and Your grace. Please forgive me of the ways I've allowed my own sin and selfishness to sabotage peace for myself and for others. Help me trust You through the storms of life. Help my faith in You inspire faith in others. Help me be an instrument of Your peace in my relationships and home.

In Jesus's name, amen.

We will experience God's peace when we make Him the authority over every part of our lives.

DAY 14

Teach Your Children the Path of Wisdom

"Lead your children onto the right path, and even when they're older, they'll still be guided by the lessons you taught them."
PROVERBS 22:6

There are so many voices in the world competing for children's attention. If you're a parent, I'm sure there are times you feel overwhelmed by the pressures of raising kids in an age of so much rebellion and confusion. Parenting a child is one of the greatest privileges and most challenging responsibilities a person can undertake. Thankfully, God gives parents strength and wisdom to help navigate the complexities of parenthood.

Proverbs has much to say about the lessons we should be teaching our children. One of its primary parenting themes centers around the need to teach kids discipline. The path to wisdom and the path to foolishness begin to fork in childhood, based on how a child responds to discipline. A lack of discipline in childhood often leads to a lack of wisdom in adulthood. That's why Proverbs gives stern instructions to parents: "Kids need discipline, so make sure they have it. *The painful consequences of a deserved punishment won't kill a child. In fact, the punishment might be the very thing that saves their life*" (Proverbs 23:13-14).

Discipline is about more than just punishment. However, appropriate punishment is part of the equation. The broader definition of discipline involves teaching children to embrace personal responsibility and accountability. It also requires instilling a work ethic in children that can take root early and blossom into a lifetime of diligent, honorable work. It means teaching them to remain teachable instead of being stubborn. It's cultivating the soil of their hearts so that the seeds of wisdom can begin to take root.

Discipline is important, but it's only one aspect of what kids need to learn. Just like adults, kids need a faith that is rooted in knowing and loving Jesus. Apart from Him, true wisdom and eternal life are not possible. Kids also need to know they're loved. They need to know the heart of God as a perfect Father who loves His children on their best days and their worst days. If children know they're truly and unconditionally loved, they've already learned the most important lesson you could teach them.

As a parent, extend grace to your kids and extend grace to yourself. Apart from God, no parent is perfect. There certainly are no perfect kids either. We all need grace. When you have blown it, apologize. Let your children see you take responsibility for your own mistakes. Your moral authority as a parent doesn't come from perfection. It comes first and foremost from God, who placed you in a position of parental authority. But authority itself doesn't guarantee influence. Your influence in your child's life comes primarily from your presence and your authenticity.

You have to be there for them. You also have to be honest. Your kids already know you're not perfect, but if they see you being honest about your imperfection and seeking to grow in your own life and faith, it will inspire their own desire to grow. Be present, be honest, and be loving. If you'll do those things, you'll be on the right track.

Remember that kids are always watching. They might not remember all the lessons you taught them, but they'll never forget your example. They'll never forget the times you were there for them. They'll never forget the moments you made them feel safe and loved. Each day, ask God to give you the wisdom to be a good parent because every day there will be opportunities to create moments your children will never forget.

> ### Prayer for Today
>
> Father, thank You that I can call You "Father." Thank You for being a perfect parent to imperfect children like me. Thank You for Your love. Please help me teach my children (or future children) the path of wisdom. Help me walk that path myself because I know their little feet will follow me whether I'm walking in wisdom or in foolishness. Please give me Your grace because I need it daily. Help me walk each day with Jesus and teach my kids to follow in His perfect example as well.
>
> In Jesus's name, amen.

Each day, ask God to give you the wisdom to be a good parent because every day there will be opportunities to create moments your children will never forget.

DAY 15

Your Temper Is a Tempter

> *"Don't befriend hotheads. Don't spend your time with people who are always angry and offended. Angry attitudes can become contagious and you might start adopting their bad habits."*
> PROVERBS 22:24-25

Anger itself is not a sin, but it can certainly lead to sin. Jesus was sinless, but He also experienced anger. He responded with a righteous rage when He saw moneychangers exploiting and extorting in the name of God. Jesus grew angry when He saw injustice, hypocritical behavior, and abuse.

Sometimes, anger is the appropriate response. But it's never the appropriate mindset.

We all know people who choose to live with an angry mindset. They see themselves as a perpetual victim. They scoff at all those who disagree with them. They shut their ears to wisdom. They want to punish but allow no correction or discipline to be brought to themselves. The Book of Proverbs bluntly describes this mindset as foolish. Unchecked anger will make a fool of you, and foolishness is a contagious condition.

As Christians, we're called to be kind to all people, but we're also called to have wisdom and discretion in choosing our close friends. Bad company corrupts good character. If you're always making excuses for a hot-tempered friend, eventually his or her temper will create unnecessary problems in your own life. Your desire to bail them out might come from altruistic and compassionate motives, but you're doing more harm than good. Let them face the natural consequences of their actions or they'll never learn.

If anger is an ongoing problem for you, then develop the daily discipline to express gratitude to God for all the good in your life. Get alone with Him. Meditate on His words and be reminded that you're loved just as you are. Much anger stems from unmet expectations and broken views of ourselves. When we replace those mindsets with a spirit of gratitude to God—and when we draw closer to God—His ways start to become our ways and anger will slowly be replaced by peace.

Prayer for Today

Lord, please help me have a heart like Yours. Let me be angered only by the things that anger You and help me have the wisdom to respond appropriately. Please forgive me for the sinful and angry mindsets I've carried. Help me replace those mindsets with Your truth and Your wisdom. Please fill my heart with Your peace, presence, and promises so anger is not my first response to unmet expectations. Please give me the wisdom to know which relationships are causing contagious anger in my life. Show me how to create safe boundaries that protect everyone involved. Help me be a peacemaker in a world full of rage.

In Jesus's name, amen.

Bad company corrupts good character.

DAY 16

Pay Attention to the Right Voices

> *"Pay attention and listen closely to the sayings of the wise. Turn your heart to what I teach; it's a gift when you keep wisdom in your heart and have wise words ready on your lips. I'm teaching you this wisdom so that your trust will be in the Lord. I have written thirty sayings for you, sayings of guidance and knowledge, teaching you to be honest and to speak the truth with integrity. These words will help you bring truth to the people in your life."*
> PROVERBS 22:17-21

This Scripture begins with two simple words: "Pay attention." This is a call to refocus on what really matters. The object of your attention will eventually become a compass directing your life. When I tell my own sons to pay attention, I'm trying to help them snap out of the stupor of mindless video games or stop feeding on our culture's mental junk food.

We have a real enemy in the world. Satan isn't a guy wearing red tights with a pitchfork. He's a deceiver who subtly tries to discourage us and distract us from God's plans and promises. When left to drift on autopilot, we're all susceptible to being numbed, discouraged, deceived, and distracted by the world's messages. We need to wake up!

Stop paying attention only to the messages of this world. Stop giving in to your own doubts, worries, and uncertainties. Stop shaping your worldview solely with what you see on social media and television.

We must also pay attention to the right advisers. Solomon's son Rehoboam split the kingdom by not listening to the sage advice of older advisers. He only trusted his peers who told him what he wanted to hear. The results were disastrous. We must seek the voices of the wise to speak in our lives. *"A nation will crumble with a lack of guidance, but with many wise counselors, there is success"* (Proverbs 11:14).

Above all voices, we need to pay attention to God's promises and commands. God is the only perfect advisor. His advice will always be correct. Get alone with Him. Turn off the noise of the world. Refocus your thoughts on His promises. You're doing this right now simply by carving out time to take part in a Bible-based devotional. Let this good decision—the one you've already made today—give way to other good decisions.

Pay attention to what God is doing all around you. He promises that we'll find Him when we seek Him with all our heart. He wants to be found by you. He's waiting. He's putting evidence of His presence all around you. He's showing you opportunities to serve others for His glory. He's inviting you to join Him in world-changing work. The opportunities are there if you'll be led by prayer, and if you'll pay attention to His promptings.

Prayer for Today

Father, thank You for Your love. Thank You that You don't make Your wisdom a mystery to us but show us in Your Word what You desire and how we should live. Help me pay attention today. Help me see clearly what You're doing all around me, so that I may join You there. Help me walk the path of wisdom and not be distracted by the world's false messages. Help me see and choose the narrow road of wisdom and life instead of the broad road of destruction. Thank You for guiding me.

In Jesus's name, amen.

Pay attention to what God is doing all around you.

DAY 17

Protect the Powerless

> *"Never take advantage of the poor. Never exploit the needy in court. The Lord is the defender who will take up their case protecting their rights and opposing all those who would abuse or disregard the poor."*
> PROVERBS 22:22-23

God's value system is different from the world's value system. When the prophet Samuel was searching for the next King of Israel, he overlooked the scrawny shepherd boy named David in favor of other men who looked the part. The Lord reminded Samuel that while the world may look at the outer appearance, God is not impressed with superficialities. God looks at the heart.

One of Jesus's most sobering parables is the story of how God will ultimately divide the righteous from the unrighteous based on how they had treated the poor and marginalized. Jesus tells us that whatever we do for the poor—whether it's helping them or exploiting them—we're ultimately doing it to Him. He's bluntly telling us that we can't say we love Him while having complete disregard for our brothers and sisters in need.

To have a heart like Jesus, we must be willing to care for people the world might overlook. There's no such thing as an "insignificant" person to God, so there should be no such thing as an "insignificant" person to us. All are precious in His sight and made in His own image. In Jesus's earthly ministry, He showed us the heart of God for the poor, the powerless, the disenfranchised, the imprisoned, the forgotten, and the marginalized.

In different ways and in different seasons of our own lives, we've all fallen into one or more of these categories. We've all been spiritually poor or financially poor. We've all been overlooked. We've all experienced injustice. In those moments of our own powerlessness, what we prayed others would do to help us is exactly what we should be doing to help others.

Use whatever influence you have to help those without influence. Use your voice to speak for those who can't speak for themselves. Recognize that your resources—and even your very life—aren't your possessions. These all belong to God, and they've been temporarily entrusted to your stewardship. Manage those resources well to provide for your own family, but also remember the needs of the poor. One of the purest acts of faith is to do good for those who can do nothing to repay us.

"Speak up for the voiceless. Ensure justice for the oppressed. Stand up for the helpless and make sure they receive justice" (Proverbs 31:8-9).

Prayer for Today

Jesus, please help me see Your face in the faces of the poor and marginalized I'm often tempted to judge, overlook, or even exploit. Help me see the dignity and sacred value in every human being—especially those the world has devalued. Please give me a heart to help those in need. Give me discernment to know how I can best help and let me be part of the solution instead of part of the problem. Thank You for loving me even in my own spiritual poverty. Thank You for giving Your life on the cross for me, though I could do nothing to repay You. Your love inspires me to love. Your compassion inspires compassion within me. Through Your Holy Spirit, please equip me to be a voice to the voiceless and to be Your hands and feet to a world in need. Let my simple acts of service point more people to Your heart.

In Jesus's name, amen.

There's no such thing as an "insignificant" person to God, so there should be no such thing as an "insignificant" person to us.

DAY 18

Financial Freedom

> *"Don't make expensive commitments or get yourself deep into debt. If you start missing payments, you could end up losing everything you have."*
> PROVERBS 22:26-27

Most modern advertising is designed to sell us stuff we don't need and can't afford. Since marketers are good at their jobs, many of us have taken the bait and overextended ourselves. Once overextended, we learn the painful lesson that no possession is worth a lack of peace. Debt can become a form of slavery, but God wants you to live with freedom.

When God warns us against unnecessary debt, it's not to limit us. Like all God's guidelines, this warning exists for our protection. He wants us to experience freedom and uninhibitedly live the full and abundant life Jesus brings us. When we choose to live with fiscal discipline, we're making an investment into our family's future freedoms. When we take on debt, we're limiting our family's future freedoms.

Every wise financial decision you make creates future opportunities, but every foolish financial decision restricts future opportunities. Make financial choices today that your future self will thank you for making. When you choose discipline today, you're free to live with generosity and abundance in the future instead of selfishness and scarcity.

Some people have misinterpreted the Bible to say that money is evil.

That's not true. 1 Timothy 6:10 says the love of money is the root of all kinds of evil, but we're also told that God has given us the ability to create wealth and the responsibility to manage resources with wisdom. Poverty is not a sin. Wealth is not a sin. What's sinful is to worship money, misuse money, or trade your freedoms in exchange for unnecessary debts.

When you allow God's Word to be your chief financial advisor—as well as your chief advisor in *all* areas of life—you'll be walking the path of wisdom. God wants you to have peace in your finances. The Bible also says God wants you to be able to leave an inheritance to your grandchildren. If you want a financial legacy of peace, prosperity, and kingdom-minded generosity, then submit to the Bible's money principles instead of the world's broken pattern of greed and discontentment.

Prayer for Today

Lord, help me trust You with my finances. Give me the faith and the discipline to be generous in my giving, wise in my investments, humble in my successes, and obedient to Your Word. I recognize that all money belongs to You and whatever I have is only temporarily entrusted to me. Help me be a wise steward of those resources. Thank You for giving me the strength and ability to earn an income. Help me be thankful for what I have. Let my ambition for more be rooted in Christ-centered motives and not in my own pride. Help me create a multi-generational legacy of financial freedom for my family and help me remember that my self-worth has nothing to do with my net worth.

In Jesus's name, amen.

Every wise financial decision you make creates future opportunities, but every foolish financial decision restricts future opportunities.

DAY 19

Develop Your Skills

> *"Being skilled and disciplined in your work opens doors of opportunity. Those who excel in their field will work alongside leaders and those with great influence."*
> PROVERBS 22:28

The Bible has so much to teach us about work. We're taught not to seek our identity in work because we can't be defined solely by a job title. We're also taught that work is important. When done with excellence, it can be an act of worship.

The passage from Proverbs challenges you to work hard at what you're doing and also to work hard at getting better. Don't settle for less than your best. You might be able to milk the time clock and still get paid by just going through the motions, but you'll never get ahead that way. Strive to maximize your potential by developing the skills God gave you.

Ambition can become dangerous when it's fueled by selfish and prideful motivations, but ambition can be a very good thing when our motives are pure. God wants His children in positions of leadership and influence. He wants our good deeds to shine before others so that we may use that influence to serve our communities and point people toward the goodness of God.

If you don't work outside the home, this verse is a challenge to improve as a parent, homemaker, friend, volunteer, or anything else you choose to do. Work doesn't require a paycheck to be sacred. Work of all kinds, from changing diapers to mopping floors to leading corporations, can be sacred work when we do it to serve others and give glory to God.

If you have a gift with organization, then read books and take on new projects that will help you become even more organized. If you're gifted with your hands, then search for a mentor who can apprentice you in new disciplines. If you're a full-time mom, then seek the wisdom of mothers who have devoted their lives to bringing up children. In whatever you do, always be willing to keep learning. Always be willing to share what you're learning with those who could benefit from your mentorship.

Start viewing your home and office as sacred places. They are every bit as sacred as a church service on Sundays. You are a temple of the Holy Spirit. Jesus lives within you from the moment you reach out to Him in faith and receive His grace. Jesus goes with you into your job. Jesus goes with you into your home. You're representing Christ in everything you do.

Once you realize this truth, everything you put your hands to becomes sacred work, and you'll want to continue to excel at it for God's glory.

Develop Your Skills

Prayer for Today

Lord, thank You for giving me unique skills and abilities. Please give me the discipline to develop those skills. Help me keep improving in all parts of my life. Don't let prideful motivations creep in and attempt to wreck what You're doing through me. In all things, help me work with a pure heart, seeking to please You more than I seek to please any human boss. Please give me more influence in my work and community. Help me leverage that influence for the good of others and for Your glory.

In Jesus's name, amen.

Work of all kinds, from changing diapers to mopping floors to leading corporations, can be sacred work when we do it to serve others and give glory to God.

DAY 20

Don't Overdo It

> "Listen to wisdom, my children, and get your hearts in the right place. Don't go partying with people who are addicted to wine and overindulgence. Gluttons and drunks become poor and laziness is their legacy."
> PROVERBS 23:19-21

Alcohol is a hot-button issue in many Christian circles. Some denominational traditions believe that all alcohol consumption is sinful. Most Christians around the world believe that Jesus made and drank real wine and that alcohol consumption is fine in moderation. Regardless of your personal convictions on the issue, Proverbs consistently and clearly teaches one lesson on alcohol: It's that immense damage can result from allowing alcohol as an unhealthy influence in your life.

A few verses after the passage above, we're given this strong warning about the dangers of drunkenness: "Who has headaches? Who has regrets? Who has animosity? Who has stress? Who has heartache? Who has anger? Who has bruises and bloodshot eyes? It's those who love the frequent the bars. It's those who are always looking for a drink. Yes, the drink might feel good for a moment, but in the end, it leaves you hurting. Your vision will be blurry, your mind will be foggy. You'll feel seasick like a sailor in a storm. You'll have an arrogant and dangerous mindset that says, "Go ahead and hit me! I can't feel a thing. I'm bulletproof. Where can I find another drink?" (Proverbs 23:29-35)

Scripture makes it clear that we should proceed very carefully with alcohol. Like many Christians, you may believe having a drink or two is a way to celebrate life, experience the purported health benefits of moderate alcohol consumption and enjoy one of the many freedoms given by God. If so, be sure to exercise caution. Don't let that freedom slowly turn into a prison. Jesus gave His very life to ensure your freedom, so don't sabotage it through foolish choices. Any form of addiction steals your freedom, and sometimes we think we're in control when we're actually losing control.

If you've developed unbalanced habits around alcohol (or anything else for that matter), then take action. Don't wait. Pause the habit altogether for a period of time. If you feel incapable of stopping completely, then it's a sign you need outside help and accountability. Don't let your pride hold you back from seeking the help you need. Reaching out for help is a sign of wisdom, not weakness.

Also be aware of friends and loved ones who might be falling into dangerous habits related to alcohol. Be careful to not cause them to stumble deeper into these habits. Be willing to ask difficult questions and point out troubling patterns. Those conversations are not easy, but Proverbs tells us that one of the hallmarks of a true friend is someone who loves enough to speak a difficult truth.

Prayer for Today

Lord, thank You for the freedoms You've given us. Please never let me misuse those freedoms and become imprisoned by unhealthy habits. Let no addiction take hold of me or my family. Please give me the wisdom to stay accountable, realizing that anyone can fall into addiction when no accountability is present. If I ever do find myself in a place where a habit has become an addiction, help me see it clearly. Give me the strength to reach out for help. Help me also be a source of strength for my friends and family and never one who causes them to stumble into sin.

In Jesus's name, amen.

Jesus gave His very life to ensure your freedom, so don't sabotage it through foolish choices.

DAY 21

Honor Those Who Have Sacrificed for You

> *"Keep learning from your father; he gave you life. Don't push away your mother when she is old. Pursue the truth, wisdom and insight as great treasures worthy of great sacrifice. The parent of a righteous child has a joyful heart. A parent's greatest treasure is having a child grow in wisdom and integrity. May your parents experience this kind of rich blessing as a result of your choices."*
> PROVERBS 23:22-25

One of the Ten Commandments is devoted to our duty in honoring our parents. Apart from our Heavenly Father, no parent is perfect. Despite every parent's inherent imperfections, when we give them our lifelong honor and respect, we're putting wisdom into actions and securing a multi-generational blessing.

As this passage from Proverbs points out, part of honoring our parents lies in living a life of honor and integrity. When you choose to embody the positive lessons they taught you, they experience a rich blessing and the fulfillment of the dreams and prayers they've had for you since you were born. Honor your parents and honor God by choosing to live a life of integrity and wisdom.

Another aspect of honoring parents involves forgiveness. Your parents weren't perfect. There were times they made mistakes. Perhaps some of those mistakes caused you great pain. Forgiveness doesn't excuse sin, but it entrusts those past wounds to God's hands. This makes healing possible in your own heart and in your relationships with those who hurt you. If it's within your power to rebuild a broken bridge to your parents, then be the one to start extending grace. In doing so, you're walking the path of wisdom.

It's important to note that, in adulthood, honoring your parents no longer means obeying them. Your primary loyalty must be to God. Your secondary loyalty, if you're married, must be to your spouse. God is the one who established this hierarchy of loyalty. If you have a parent who desires an unnatural level of control over your life, you may have to lovingly establish firm boundaries. Even when boundaries need to be established, you can still show honor through your words *to* your parents and your words *about* your parents.

Your parents (and other mentors in your life) have done much more for you than you've seen with your own eyes. The prayers they have prayed for you and the sacrifices they've made for you have blessed you in ways that can never be calculated or adequately repaid. You are standing on the shoulders of giants. Give them honor. Show them gratitude. Live a life of integrity and you'll make their hearts happy. You'll also be honoring your Father in heaven.

Prayer for Today

Father, please help me honor You and honor my parents through my gratitude, respect and integrity. Help me live a life that becomes an answer to the prayers they prayed for me from the time I was a child. Thank You for my parents and for the mentors You've placed in my life over the years. I know there have been countless sacrifices made on my behalf and countless prayers prayed for me. Give me a spirit of gratitude as I reflect often on those sacrifices. Help me live in a way that brings honor to my family and glory to You.

In Jesus's name, amen.

Honor your parents and honor God by choosing to live a life of integrity and wisdom.

DAY 22

Always Tell the Truth

"An honest answer is as sweet as a kiss."
PROVERBS 24:26

To walk the path of wisdom means you must also walk the path of truth. The path to foolishness is paved with lies, but wisdom requires a lifelong commitment to honesty. God has no greater joy than to see His children walking in truth.

One of the main themes in Proverbs is the importance of honesty in all parts of life. There are Scriptures about honesty in business, honesty in courtrooms and honesty in relationships. The poetry of this verse from Proverbs uses the word "kiss" to remind us that honesty is about more than just being factually correct. Honesty is an expression of love.

Since the truth requires love, we must be careful not to speak cruelty cloaked in truth. Honesty is not a license to be everyone's critic. Be an encourager. The world has plenty of critics already. Let your words be true—but let them also be loving, encouraging and compassionate.

Being loving and kind doesn't mean you'll never have to share a difficult truth. Proverbs also tells us that a true friend will sometimes have to speak truth that's hard to say and hard to hear. In those delicate moments, be honest and direct. Make sure your motives are based purely on helping the friend you're admonishing. You must also be humble enough to hear honest words of correction spoken to you. Honesty requires humility both in how we speak and in how we listen.

Honesty is also not a license to gossip or to have unfiltered conversations about others. It might be "true" that you heard something about someone's life, but that does not give you license to share it. Don't be a gossiper and don't befriend gossipers. Anyone who will gossip *to* you will also gossip *about* you.

We might try to hide the ostensibly innocent motives of our gossip behind a feigned desire to help the person we're talking about, but gossiping is always dangerous. Proverbs has blunt warnings for those who would justify gossip. Many verses warn against the sin of gossip. Others simply point out the consequences of it, like the Proverb that states, *"A fire dies out without wood to fuel it and fighting dies out without gossip to fuel it"* (Proverbs 26:20).

Choose to live a life where your words are always true and your words are always building others up instead of tearing them down. Choose to be honest in your business dealings, even when it might cost you something. Speaking the truth—even when it costs us to do so—is a beautiful expression of our faith and proof of our integrity. God will always honor that kind of costly honesty. The truth is always worth the price.

Prayer for Today

Lord, thank You that You are always honest. You are the Way, the Truth and the Life. You, Jesus, are the very embodiment of Truth. Please help me live my life walking in the path of truth and honesty. Forgive me for the times I've been dishonest, cruel with my words or a gossip. I know words and motives have power and there have been times my words and motives have been impure. Thank You for Your grace. Help me commit my words and my motives to your perfect standard of truth, even when the truth costs me something. Let me never fear the sacrifices that must sometimes be made in the pursuit of truth and integrity.

In Jesus' name, amen.

Be an encourager. The world has plenty of critics already.

DAY 23

Criticism Won't Kill You

*"To the one who listens and learns from it,
constructive criticism is as valuable as solid gold."*
PROVERBS 25:12

Nobody likes to hear criticism. But criticism can be a refining fire that helps strengthen us and burns away our imperfections. One of the primary distinctions between the wise and the foolish is in how they handle criticism. The fool will scoff at any form of correction, but a wise person will use the critic—regardless of the critic's motives—to become even wiser.

If you desire to have influence in any part of life, you must know this: Criticism is the price of influence. The more influence you attain, the more criticism you will have to endure. Many people have hidden from their life's calling simply because they did not have the courage to endure the criticisms that will always come when we step out in faith into all God has for us.

Avoiding criticism is a futile effort because even if you hide from it, criticism will find you. In a world full of scoffers, critics and know-it-alls, everyone seems to have an opinion (usually negative) about almost everything. We can be dragged down by this pervasive negativity, but we must also train our ears to find the important truths hidden within the criticism.

There are essentially two types of critics who will come into your life. The first type has no motive except to hurt you. Their words are like daggers, and they want to discredit and discourage you. Remember that these negative people are usually wounded in some way. Their venom and vitriol directed toward you is really just a way for them to mask their own internal wounds. Pray for these people, but don't let their words make you second-guess your calling or your abilities.

The second type of critic is the person who cares about you and wants you to get better. Their motives are usually pure, even when their words might seem harsh. Guard your heart when you hear their criticisms. Don't be discouraged. At the same time, have the humble spirit to learn from their perspective. Learn to see your own blind spots. Learn to be teachable. The moment you stop listening to correction is the moment you stop growing.

Prayer for Today

Father, please help me always remain teachable. First and foremost, let me stay teachable when you bring correction into my life through the Holy Spirit and the truth of your Word. Let me humbly receive the loving correction You bring all Your beloved children. Also, help me remain open to constructive criticism from other people. Never let me grow discouraged or despondent because of the negativity of scoffers, but also help me keep my ears open to the constructive correction I need to hear. Help me be thankful and not defensive when someone has the courage to offer me constructive criticism. Keep teachable and growing through every season of life.

In Jesus's name, amen.

Criticism is the price of influence. The more influence you attain, the more criticism you will have to endure.

DAY 24

Be Sensitive to Those Who Are Hurting

> *"Trying to force a grieving person to cheer up is as insensitive as taking away someone's coat in a snowstorm or pouring vinegar into a wound."*
> PROVERBS 25:20

There's a time to "cheer up" someone who is feeling discouraged, but when a loved one is in a time of intense grief or sadness, they need you to honor their pain. Honoring someone's pain means acknowledging that they're in a season of deep difficulties and choosing to help them through it by being present. It means letting them set the emotional tone. When they feel like laughing, be there to laugh with them. When they feel like crying, be a safe place for them to share their tears.

A young man lost his young wife to cancer. In an instant, his dreams were crushed, his bride was gone, and he was suddenly a single father of two young children. The first year after her death became a "dark night of the soul" for him as he experienced the depths of human pain. While many people did their best to encourage him, few could relate to the tragedy he was experiencing.

Eventually someone asked what had brought him the most hope during his darkest days. "When someone is hurting, don't try to cheer them up by telling them it's going to be okay," the young man said. "Just be with them in their pain until *they're* ready to say it's going to be okay."

He was describing the ministry of presence. In our most painful moments, we gain strength from the presence of our loved ones. Don't avoid your loved ones who are hurting. Don't be intimidated by not knowing what to say. There is power in presence. In our pain, we rarely remember the words people say to us, but we never forget who showed up to be there with us.

If you're in a season of pain, know that God is with you. Of course, God is always with us, but the Scriptures promise that He is especially close to the brokenhearted. He comes on a rescue mission for us when our hearts feel broken and our souls feel crushed by the weight of tragedy. He promises to wipe every tear from our eyes. One day, He has promised to set all things right and make all things new. Because of Jesus, our pain is temporary, and our joy will be eternal.

If you're in a season of pain, please also extend grace to your friends. Pain can warp our thinking and make us quick to take offense at our friends' absence or their inability to take our pain away. People are flawed and imperfect. During your moments of pain, choose to believe the best in your loved ones—even if they're not "there for you" in the ways you want them to be. You never know all they're carrying in their own life. Jesus is the only perfect friend. Everyone else, including you, will be a disappointing friend at times.

Don't run from people in the times of their pain, and don't run from people when you are the one who is hurting. Healing happens in community. We need God and we need each other. When we carry each other's burdens, the load gets much lighter.

Prayer for Today

Jesus, thank You for coming to earth to experience sadness and pain so You can relate to us in our times of grief. Thank You for being present with me in my own pain. Help me be present and encouraging to my friends and relatives when they're hurting. Give me the courage to be present with them in their pain and to be an extension of Your hands and feet in their life during those critical moments. Help me be a good friend. Help me have good friends in my time of need. Thank You for being a friend who is always there for me.

In Jesus's name, amen.

In our pain, we rarely remember the words people say to us, but we never forget who showed up to be there with us.

DAY 25

Learn from Your Mistakes

> *"Just like a dog will return to its own vomit,*
> *a fool will return to his foolish choices."*
> PROVERBS 26:11

This verse is intentionally graphic in its description of a disgusting action. If you've ever owned a dog, then you've probably seen your pet regurgitate food and then lick it up again, as if it has somehow become a delicious delicacy. As humans, the thought of this is sickening. But this Scripture reminds us that, through our repeated sins, bad habits and foolish mindsets, we're perpetually returning to something even more repulsive than vomit. This vivid imagery isn't just hyperbole. It's a wake-up call.

You might imagine that this verse is primarily about poking fun at other people's foolishness and not our own. That wouldn't be consistent with Scripture, since even Jesus warned us to be aware of the plank of wood in our own eye before we worried about the speck of sawdust in someone else's eye. The purpose of this verse is to bring sobering self-assessment into our own lives. What is the proverbial "vomit" you keep returning to? What are the unhealthy habits you need to change?

Sometimes our unhealthy habits and foolish quirks are more obvious than others. If you're dealing with an addiction of some kind, the imagery of this verse might hit uncomfortably close to home. Perhaps you're well aware of your issue but you can't seem to pull away from it. Despite your feelings of self-loathing and helplessness, you can't seem to break free. In cases like these, you need to reach out and get help. The only foolish way to deal with an addiction is to think you can beat it on your own. Get the help you need to break free.

At other times, our repetitive and self-destructive habits may be harder to spot. They may be tied to a mindset. Perhaps your thoughts get stuck in a negative mental loop and the "vomit" in your situation is a thought process. You can't get out of a cycle of negativity. In those cases, you must take your thoughts captive and renew your mind with the truths of Scripture. Meditate on God's Word instead of fueling your mind with the world's toxic messages. Add long periods of silence and stillness into your day so God can do His work without competing with the noise of the world.

Remember that every sin begins in the mind, and every positive action begins in the mind, too. You must be the gatekeeper of your mind, choosing which thoughts and images are allowed to enter and which ones must leave. God will help you in this mental exercise if you'll let Him. Like all parts of life, you don't have to do it alone. The Holy Spirit is there to guide you, strengthen you, and empower you.

Prayer for Today

Lord, please forgive me for all the ways I've struggled with repetitive sins and foolish habits. Please help me break free. Please bring conviction to help me clearly see the toxic parts of my life, as well as any mindsets which might have become blind spots to me. Guide me toward healthier thoughts and habits. Help me stay committed to positive habits such as daily time alone with You in prayer and reading from Your Word. Thank You for caring about every detail of my life.
   In Jesus's name, amen.

What is the proverbial "vomit" you keep returning to? What are the unhealthy habits you need to change?

DAY 26

Don't Pick Fights

> *"Inserting yourself into someone else's argument is as foolish and reckless as yanking a wolf's ears."*
> PROVERBS 26:17

We live in an age when everyone seems to have an opinion about everything. Our interconnectivity through technology has given people a platform where they can weigh in on every situation. We've bought into the dangerous myth that our opinion always needs to be shared and every disagreement requires taking sides. This prideful mindset perpetuates conflict rather than bringing any form of resolution.

The only time it's appropriate to insert yourself, uninvited, into someone's situation is when you are ministering and not meddling. Knowing the difference between the two can be complicated sometimes. Jesus gives a vivid example of what uninvited ministering looks like in his famous Parable of the Good Samaritan. In the story, a man is beaten and robbed and left for dead. Several religious leaders pass by the bloody victim on the road but choose not to get involved. A foreigner from Samaria— with plenty of excuses not to stop— selflessly decides to serve this victim by sacrificing his own time and financial resources.

Jesus hails this "Good Samaritan" as the quintessential example of what it means to be a good neighbor and to show love for others. When given the opportunity to serve selflessly, we should always do it. When we see someone in desperate need and it is within our power to help, we must put our faith into action.

The difference between the Good Samaritan scenario and inserting yourself into someone else's affairs in a negative way largely comes down to your own motives. When you're motivated by selfish pride, you'll find yourself feeling entitled to correct others. When you're motivated by love, you'll find yourself feeling compelled to serve others. Love brings healing and unity, but pride brings destruction and division.

Don't let argumentative people bait you into senseless fights and arguments. Be kind even to unkind people. Your kindness isn't a reflection of their character. Your kindness is a reflection of God's character. He is loving and patient with us even at our worst moments. As ambassadors of Christ on earth, make it your mission to be like Him in all situations.

Jesus was the perfect example of knowing when to intervene and when to stay out of an argument. Jesus helped all those in His path who needed His help. He lovingly taught all those who came to Him with a desire to learn, but He also never fell into the trap of wasting His time and energy debating with those who only wanted to argue. When people tried to entrap Him in no-win situations, Jesus would always show love and speak truth, but also showed the wisdom and restraint to walk away.

When someone needs your help, let love compel you to help. When someone baits you into an argument, let wisdom compel you to walk away. When you're not sure whether a complicated situation requires your intervention or your absence, ask the Holy Spirit to guide you. When you allow your heart to be guided by God's principles and His Spirit, you'll have discernment in those moments.

Do your best to live at peace with all people but recognize that some people will refuse to live at peace with you. In those cases, pray for them and love them from a distance. Don't sink to the level of those who want to sling mud. Always take the high road.

Prayer for Today

Lord, in a world with so much outrage, please help me be an ambassador of peace. Help me have the courage to help those who truly need my help. Help me have the wisdom and restraint to walk away from arguments that don't concern me. Guide my steps, my words, and my actions. Thank You, Jesus, for the perfect example You gave to us through Your own life. Let Your Holy Spirit guide me make those same wise decisions and use my life to point others toward You in the process.

In Jesus's name, amen.

Be kind even to unkind people. Your kindness isn't a reflection of their character. Your kindness is a reflection of God's character.

DAY 27

Let Others Do Your Bragging for You

> *"Don't brag about the future since you don't know what will happen tomorrow. Let other people do your bragging for you. If you sing your own praises, you'll be singing a solo."*
> PROVERBS 27:1-2

The world's definition of success seems to be tied up in endless self-promotion and self-aggrandizement. God's definition of success is based on our faithfulness and not our fame. When we buy into the world's version of success, we'll look for every imaginable opportunity to brag, name-drop, and shine the spotlight on our personal brands because we think that's what it takes to get ahead. When we find rest and peace in God as the Keeper of our life and purpose, we have the confidence to reject the superficial rituals of the world.

Most bragging, at its core, is a cry for validation from a broken and insecure heart. Ironically, we act most puffed-up when we feel most empty inside. When we see others bragging, our initial response might be to roll our eyes and pass judgment on their immaturity. While we shouldn't approve of anyone's bragging, we should also have compassion. Most bragging stems more from brokenness than from pride.

Perhaps you weren't loved and validated as a child by your parents. The adult wounds left from childhood brokenness can leave lasting scars. We might end up as braggarts and approval junkies, hoping the accolades of the world will somehow make up for the emptiness we feel. What you and I need to remember is that no amount of praise from the world can ever fill that void. Only God can fill that void. He is the source of your wholeness.

Once you've decided to root your identity in Christ, you'll find yourself far less impacted by the world's praise or the world's criticisms. You won't have the same need to receive credit or praise. You'll be content to do your work faithfully, knowing God sees it all—and His opinion of you counts more than the combined weight of all the world's opinions.

You are loved by God. Let that sink in. He sees you. He knows every detail of your life. He's seen you at your very best and your very worst, and He loves you more than you can possibly imagine. Once that sinks in, it will set you free.

If you're doing anything worth bragging about, others will eventually do your bragging for you. This will be a much more compelling endorsement of your work because it comes from others' lips and not your own. When you brag on the work of others instead of your own work, you'll find your choice to be a cheerleader for others will bring joy to them *and* to you. Don't spend your whole life chasing the fickle praise of this world when you already have the unending love of God.

> ### *Prayer for Today*
>
> Lord, thank You for loving me. Help me root my identity in Your love and not in the opinions of others. Forgive me for the times I've let my sinful pride motivate me to brag and draw the spotlight to myself. Help me be humble enough to point the spotlight back on You, and to also give encouragement to others. Help me be content in Your love, knowing Your opinion of my work is the only one that counts for eternity. Help me pursue wisdom more than fame, and service more than the spotlight. In Jesus's name, amen.

Once you've decided to root your identity in Christ, you'll find yourself far less impacted by the world's praise or the world's criticisms.

DAY 28

Confession Brings Healing

"People who try to cover up their sins and scandals will not prosper, but if they confess and turn from them, they'll find mercy."
PROVERBS 28:13

When selfish pride is our motivation, we are tempted to protect our image at all costs. When our image becomes threatened because of our sin and inevitable imperfections, we are tempted to shift blame or spin the story instead of humbly admitting fault. Confessing and apologizing for our mistakes requires courage and wisdom. Making excuses or blaming others for our mistakes shows cowardice and foolishness.

The Bible gives many examples of those who have chosen wisely and others who have chosen foolishly when confronted with their own sin. A foolish example is when Ananias and Sapphira, a married couple in the Book of Acts, were caught in a lie. Instead of confessing, they continued to perpetuate the lie. Their stubborn dishonesty and pride cost them their very lives. Their story is a sobering reminder that a refusal to speak truth and accept personal responsibility carries consequences.

A positive example in the Bible is when a courageous young woman named Rahab decided to turn from her sinful life of prostitution to align herself with God's principles. She left a life of dishonor and was greatly honored as a result. She risked her life to help God's people attain a strategic military victory. Eventually, she married and became the matriarch in a line of Israel's greatest kings. She's even listed in the earthly lineage of Jesus Himself.

The world's response will sometimes mirror God's merciful principle here, but there are also times when the world's response won't match God's response. Obviously, we've seen occasions when a leader is perpetually embroiled in scandals, never takes responsibility, and always shifts blame. Yet he continues to increase in power or popularity. There are other times when someone will humbly admit fault but still becomes the victim of "cancel culture" or other forms of targeted harassment. The world's response isn't always the best indication of God's response.

The Bible tells us that these types of injustices will happen in life. We're also told not to be discouraged when the wicked prosper or when we see injustice of any kind. God has an eternal mindset. The temporary injustices of our world will one day be set right, once and for all. Following God's plan, even when it comes at personal cost, will ultimately bring an incalculable return of blessings.

We will experience some of those blessings in this life, but we will experience them in perfect fullness in Heaven. Live with that eternal perspective. God will always make good on His promises to reward those who confess and renounce their sin. He will always hold accountable those who conceal and deny their sin. Choose to trust Him. Know that the Lord will honor our faithfulness even when the world dishonors it.

Prayer for Today

Lord, give me the courage to admit fault. Give me the humility to recognize fault. Don't let sinful pride cloud my judgment or sabotage your plans for me. Help me extend grace to myself and also to those who have wronged me. Help me have the faith to offer forgiveness, even to those who have never asked me for it. Holding a grudge only hurts the one who holds it, so let me live freely. Forgive me for all the ways I've committed and concealed sins. Help me choose a new path. Thank You for Your forgiveness and grace.
In Jesus's name, amen.

Confessing and apologizing for our mistakes requires courage and wisdom. Making excuses or blaming others for our mistakes shows cowardice and foolishness.

DAY 29

Think before You Speak

> *"There is nothing more foolish than to speak before thinking about your words."*
> PROVERBS 29:20

In the New Testament, Jesus teaches that we will all be held accountable for every word we've ever spoken. He warns that our words will have the power to condemn us or to acquit us. As part of the greater Gospel narrative, we know that only Christ Himself and our faith in Him has the power to save us, but that doesn't diminish the personal responsibility we have for our words. Jesus clearly wants us to see that our words matter deeply. Every word we've ever spoken matters.

The power of our words is a repeated theme throughout all Scripture. From the beginning of time, in Genesis, we are taught that God used His words to speak the universe into existence. He then created us (men and women) in His own image, giving us power in our words as well. We must use the power of words for good and not for evil. We must use our words to build each other up and not to tear each other down.

The solution isn't to live as mute monks who are afraid to speak for fear of sinning. We must have the courage to engage in meaningful dialogues, but we must also be keenly aware of the power of words and the damages an undisciplined mouth can cause. Not every thought you have needs to be verbalized. Not every opinion you have needs to be posted on social media. There is wisdom in speaking a timely word, but there's also much wisdom in having the restraint to not speak at all.

Part of being a wise peacemaker means walking away from an argument instead of insisting on being heard. Wisdom often requires restraining your emotions instead of letting heightened emotions give fuel to thoughtless words. As the Proverbs also tell us, *"Fools give full vent to their anger, but wise people quietly restrain their anger"* (Proverbs 29:11).

This doesn't mean we should never confront others. There are certainly times when confrontation is needed. Jesus wasn't afraid to confront others and we shouldn't be either. In those moments, remember that motives matter. If you want to confront someone just to "put them in their place" or make your own voice heard, then you're on dangerous ground. If your motive is to protect everyone involved and preserve relationships by establishing healthy boundaries, then strong words are probably appropriate.

In all situations, think before you speak. Ask yourself, "Is what I'm about to say true, kind, and necessary?" Speak the truth in love. Speak with wisdom. Speak humbly. Remember that your words have power, and our speech is a direct reflection of our hearts.

Prayer for Today

Lord, thank You for giving us so much power in our words. You've trusted us with a great responsibility. Please help me have the wisdom to use the power of words in a positive way. Forgive me for all the times I've spoken with impure words or impure motives. Let every word I speak honor You and be used to build others up. Help me always practice the discipline of thinking before I speak.

In Jesus's name, amen.

We must use our words to build each other up and not to tear each other down.

DAY 30

God Is Our Protector

*"All God's promises are true.
All people who trust in Him are secure."*
PROVERBS 30:5

At the end of Jesus's famous Sermon on the Mount, He summed up His teachings with an illustration about a wise builder and a foolish builder. The wise builder built his house on a solid foundation. The foolish builder put his house on an unsteady foundation. Both houses looked good from the outside, but when the storms of life raged, only the house with a solid foundation was left standing.

The moral of Jesus's story is that our lives are being built on a foundation. We must choose whether we build our lives on a foundation of God's promises or the shifting sands of our own feelings or cultural whims. Faith in God anchors us through life's storms. Storms in life may be inevitable, but destruction is optional. Trusting in God is what makes all the difference.

Throughout the ages, followers of Christ have withstood relentless storms by holding to an even more relentless faith. In her book *The Hiding Place*, Corrie Ten Boom recounts her life inside a Nazi concentration camp, where she was sent for hiding Jewish families to save their lives during the Holocaust. She wrote about the abhorrent conditions in the camp. Despite the abuse she endured, she refused to complain and decided to trust God's promises.

She even trusted the Scripture that commands us to give thanks in all situations. Other women asked her how she could thank God for the putrid smells and the fleas and the disease in their filthy barracks. She replied that the filthy conditions kept the guards outside, which gave the women inside the freedom to openly praise God, pray, share conversations, laugh, and experience some measure of dignity and privacy.

When we choose to trust in God's promises, we will start to see God's blessings where others only see curses. We will see opportunities for ministry where others see limitations. We will see opportunities for gratitude and joy where others find excuses to complain and feel discouragement.

Trust in God's promises because they all hold true. You'll find strength in God's promises when you hide His Word in your heart. Take time to meditate on God's Word. Memorize it. Build your life on a foundation of His Word and your life will weather any storm.

Prayer for Today

Lord, thank You for keeping Your Word. Thank You that all Your promises hold true. Thank You for being the foundation where I can build my life and my hope for eternity. Thank You, Jesus, for the sacrifice You made for me. Help me trust in You with every detail of my life. Please forgive me for the many times I've taken my eyes off You and become discouraged. Remind me of Your faithfulness, so that I might cling to faith through all life's storms. I know You're always holding me.
In Jesus's name, amen.

Storms in life may be inevitable, but destruction is optional. Trusting in God is what makes all the difference.

DAY 31

A Wife of Noble Character

"Charm is superficial and beauty is temporary; but a woman who trusts the Lord will be celebrated. Honor her for all she has done. Let her noble lifestyle be esteemed by everyone."
PROVERBS 31:30-31

One of the most obvious places where the world's broken value system can be seen is in the world's treatment of women. Through a myriad of misogynistic practices through the centuries, women have been objectified and valued through a skewed, superficial lens. The Book of Proverbs saves its final words to make it clear that God honors women—and everyone else should as well.

In the secular world, one of the most pervasive misconceptions about Christianity is that it perpetuates a worldview that holds women down. The truth is that no person in the totality of human history has done more to elevate women than Jesus did during His life and ministry. In radically countercultural ways, Jesus empowered women through His words, friendship, example, grace, and healing. He even empowered women through His teachings, intentionally highlighting female heroes in many of His parables.

As Christians, we need to be leaders in honoring women. We also need to be leaders in honoring women for their honorable character above superficial qualities like physical appearance.

For women, Proverbs 31 may be a call for you to receive honor, but it's also a roadmap for the type of life and work God sees as most worthy of honor. It's a life of integrity and effort. It's a life of selfless service. For those of you who are wives and/or mothers, it's a life where your family is blessed because of all you do for them. As the woman of the house, you have a unique, God-given ability to set the climate for the entire family. Choose to create a climate of warmth, encouragement, laughter, love, and mutual support.

As husbands, we must honor our wives as the treasures they are. Jesus honored His bride (the Church) by giving His very life for her. As husbands, we are called to honor our wives with the same kind of love and selfless sacrifice Jesus displayed. Always treat each other like a treasure. If you treat your spouse like a treasure, your marriage will be a treasure. If your treat your spouse like a burden, your marriage will feel like a burden. *"The man who finds a wife finds a treasure, and he receives favor from the Lord"* (Proverbs 18:22).

Prayer for Today

Lord, help me live out the message of Proverbs 31. Help me celebrate honorable women and strive for that kind of honor in my own life. I pray my family would receive the blessings described in the Proverbs as I do my part to live out these lessons. Please give me the strength to apply these words in my heart, my home, and every part of my life. Create a generational legacy through me, where love and wisdom will spread through my example as I continue to follow You. Thank You, Jesus, for the wisdom and the grace You give us. Guide me by Your Holy Spirit to walk with You all the days of my life.

In Jesus's name, amen.

As Christians, we need to be leaders in honoring women.

NEXT STEPS

You've reached the end of this book, but I pray it's only the beginning of your journey in applying God's wisdom to every part of your life. As you continue to study God's Word, I challenge you to read one chapter from Proverbs each day as part of your daily Bible reading. If you do this, you'll complete the 31 chapters of Proverbs once every month. This daily discipline can have a profound impact on your faith, and each time you reread the wisdom of the Bible, the Holy Spirit will bring His Word to life in fresh ways for you.

In addition to the Proverbs, please explore the rest of the Bible as well. The Psalms and Gospels—New Testament stories about Jesus—are a good place to start and a good place to keep returning. We all have our favorite places in the Bible, but make sure you're exploring the totality of God's Word, from Genesis to Revelation. Every word of the Bible is God-breathed, timeless, powerful, and practical to help you in every part of life. Keep treasuring God's Word and your life will become a blessing to God and to others as you grow more like Jesus every day.

ABOUT THE AUTHOR

Dave Willis is a pastor, writer and marriage ministry leader. His books, blogs, videos, podcasts, social media channels and live events have reached millions of people worldwide. Dave and his wife, Ashley, are also part of the team at XO Marriage which is the nation's largest marriage-focused ministry. Dave and Ashley have four wonderful sons and one spoiled puppy. For additional resources, please visit www.DaveWillis.org